*To love and to be loved is
to feel the sun from both sides.*

~ **David Viscott**

Also by
Chez Raginiak

My Escape To Freedom
Learn English Without Teachers

In Love

Poems
by
Chez Raginiak

Copyright © 2010 by Chez Raginiak

All Rights Reserved. No part of this book may be used or reproduced in any manner whatsoever without the written permission of the author, with the exception of "WILL YOU BE MY AIR?" and "I WILL BE YOUR AIR." These two poems may be used in commitment ceremonies. However, I'd love to hear from you, and I will celebrate your love also—over the distance.

chez@1moment.us
(651) 775-4294

ISBN - 10: 0-9825071-3-5
ISBN - 13: 978-0-9825071-3-1

Back cover photo by Sandy Ryan

Published by Chez Raginiak
1Moment, LLC
P.O. Box 5555
Hopkins, MN 55343 USA
www.1moment.us

Printed in the U.S.A.

To you…

CONTENTS

A Wish For You — 11

We Are In Love — 13
Destinations — 15
Feeling Hearts — 17
My Dream — 19
While You Were Gone — 21
The Fire Keeps On Burning — 23
Daj Mi — 24
Give Me — 25
A Goodnight Poem — 29
To The Future Of Love — 31
Our Travelings Together — 33
You Have — 37
Where Hearts Unite — 39
I Feel Peaceful — 41
Cuando Estoy Contigo — 42
When I Am With You — 43
We Just Could Not End It — 47
Pancakes Made With Your Smile — 49
What I Wouldn't Give — 51
You Can — 53
When I Miss You — 57
Discovering You — 59
Will You Be My Air? — 61
I Will Be Your Air — 63

Final Note — 64

A WISH FOR YOU

My life hasn't been the same since the publication of my first book, *My Escape To Freedom*. What a great experience it's been! Countless emails and messages arrived from readers who identified with the triumph, pain, the journey, the discovery, and the challenges described in the pages of the book. I am thankful for every shared story, every tear, and every smile.

And now, I hope these poems help you see that our lives can blossom with flowers of love, joy, wonder, desires, and hope that the best is still ahead of us—*because it is.*

*Love is the master key that opens
the gates of happiness.*

~ Oliver Wendell Holmes

WE ARE IN LOVE

On our way from one day to another,
I held your hand in mine.
On our way from one season to another,
Our hearts were ready to meet.

"I am happy," you said.
"I feel it," I replied,
And we kissed.

Then we climbed to the top of a mountain
And spun around until
our lives started turning,
we believed that roses can be given forever,
we trusted a smile,
we could free our fantasies,
we were able to touch, touch everywhere,
we could scream over the valleys,
"We are in love!"

*In the arithmetic of love,
one plus one equals everything,
and two minus one equals nothing.*

~ **Mignon McLaughlin**

DESTINATIONS

To small villages around the world,
quiet beaches on all seas,
the cabin in the woods,
families across the ocean,
you, resting next to me.
To forgotten notes in our in-boxes,
photos strangers took of us,
songs we remember from the 80s,
me, through your simple sophistication,
you, through my handmade gifts.
To endless walks in parks,
picnics in gazebos—just before rain,
unplanned getaways—away from routines,
my szeptów* in your ear,
the goosebumps on your legs.
To the future of our children,
the love we exemplify,
the bottom of our secrets,
the love in our hearts,
the lifelines in our hands.

* whispers (*Polish*)

The heart has reasons that reason does not understand.

~ Jacques Benigne Bossuel

FEELING HEARTS

Nervous,
standing within my reach in front of people,
you let us peek into your life
through the keyhole of your words.

There was a Christmas tree in your tale,
right outside the house.
I could hear a sense of home
and a quiet sigh of longing, similar to mine.

Soon after, with no one around,
we met at your home.
This time you didn't say much.
You were calm.

Using the Christmas tree needles,
we packed the keyhole,
rested on the sofa and let our eyes talk,
knees rub,
hands clench,
lips meet,
bodies unite
—with limitless imagination,
—with endless possibility,
—with our hearts…feeling.

*Better never to have met you in my dream
than to wake and reach for hands
that are not there.*

~ Otomo No Yakamochi

MY DREAM

My dream,
where a flawless world exists—
a rousing place of pleasures,
passionate desires, and satisfied love.

In it, you,
with your lips half-open,
like a silent fog that moistens sleepy meadows,
you stroke my thirsty lips with yours.

"Don't leave!" you whisper to me at sunrise.
I wake up and kiss your still half-open lips.

*If I had a single flower for every time
I think about you,
I could walk forever in my garden.*

~ **Claudia Ghandi**

WHILE YOU WERE GONE

While you were gone
your voice echoed on bare streets of my soul.

While you were gone
your scent was with me wherever my mind rushed.

While you were gone
your smile looked at me from every mirror of hope.

While you were gone
your light hair tickled my face in my lonely dream.

While you were gone
my world was half empty.

*We find rest in those we love,
and we provide a resting place
in ourselves for those who love us.*

~ Saint Bernard of Clairvaux

THE FIRE KEEPS ON BURNING

By the fireplace,
in silence,
with the blankets on our backs and feet,
and the flames dancing in our eyes,

we listen to each other to hear our past,
look at each other to see our future,
ask of each other to understand our nows,
nurse one another to heal our wounds.

We hold each other tight to ensure we can feel,
help one another to show that we care,
encourage one another to travel our own paths,
pray for each other, so we meet in one place.

In silence,
we add logs to our fire,
and it keeps on burning
when we're together, and when we're not.

DAJ MI*

Daj mi swoje usta—
każdy pocałunek, który kładą,
bym mógł ich dotknąć,
połączyć je delikatnie z moimi ustami.

Daj mi delikatność swojej skóry—
każdą falę i ruch,
każde zgięcie i dolinę,
bym mógł cię podziwiać, czuć, pamiętać.

Daj mi szept twoich słów—
każdy dźwięk, każdą zwrotkę ze snów,
każde nocne jęknięcie i westchnienie,
bym mógł cię słyszeć, pożądać, w zachwyceniu.

Daj mi swoje najgłębsze marzenia—
wszystkie drogocenne,
te osiągalne i nieosiągalne,
to cię przekonam, że wszystko jest realne.

* *(Polish version)*

GIVE ME

Give me your lips—
every kiss they deliver,
so I can touch them,
unite them gently with my lips.

Give me the softness of your skin—
every wave and motion,
every curve and valley,
so I can admire you, feel you, remember.

Give me the whisper of your words—
every sound, every verse,
every midnight moan and sigh,
so I can hear you, desire you, delight.

Give me your deepest dreams—
every precious one,
those reachable and unreachable,
so I can show you that everything is possible.

Jesteśmy liśćmi jednej gałęzi,
kroplami jednego morza,
kwiatami jednego ogrodu.

~ Jean-Baptiste Henry Lacordaire

We are the leaves of one branch,
the drops of one sea,
the flowers of one garden.

~ **Jean-Baptiste Henry Lacordaire**

*You know you're in love when
you can't fall asleep
because reality is finally better
than your dreams.*

~ Dr. Seuss

A GOODNIGHT POEM

A goodnight poem
that calms your mind and massages your feet—

A goodnight poem
that promises adoring thoughts, and more at sunrise—

A goodnight poem,
so I remember how it feels to give,
and you, how to receive
words of pleasure and nearness—

A goodnight poem
filled with our lips, love, and hope.

*I like the dreams of the future
better than the history of the past.*

~ **Thomas Jefferson**

TO THE FUTURE OF LOVE

On a frigid afternoon,
by your shivering car,
your warm heart tightly guarded your
> secret dreams,
> dormant desires,
> untold wishes.

Days later, you sat with me on a frozen bench
not knowing what to say,
hesitant to pull out of your timid mind
> your intricate life,
> frozen expectations,
> an elephant guilt remaining a taboo.

The next time we met was winter again.
You were still and quiet like an ice-closed rose.
Quivering, you breathed out a warm wish
> to fly away from your unfulfilled past,
> through the sky of spirit,
> to the future of love.

*Your feet will bring you
to where your heart is.*

~ Irish Proverb

OUR TRAVELINGS TOGETHER

Over the oceans,
over coatings of the dust on our past,
to the safaris of Africa,
Rocky Mountains of Canada,
lakes of Northern Minnesota,
Camelbacks of Arizona.

To the future envisioned on our lonely nights,
to places where no intimidation or manipulation
can poison our breakfasts at home,
lunches in the park, and dinners on the patio.

Over the borders of our patience and tolerance,
over the rivers of chances flowing in our hands,
to the birthdays of our brothers and sisters,
to foreign accents more familiar each day.

To my pajama top shared with you that night,
the feeling of your skin on my face,
a slow dance that should last forever,
a fresh taste of our first moments,
the unhesitant words of love,
the perfect beginnings
of our travelings together.

Kocham cię nie za to, kim jesteś,
ale za to, kim ja się staję,
kiedy jestem z tobą.

~ Angeleaknewin Roy Croft

*I love you not because of who you are,
but because of who I am
when I am with you.*

~ **Angeleaknewin Roy Croft**

*What is not started today
is never finished tomorrow.*

~ Johann Wolfgang von Goethe

YOU HAVE

You have only one road to travel, yours.
Face it.

You have only one life to live, yours.
Free it.

You have only one dream to dream, yours.
Fulfill it.

You have only one soul to share, yours.
Nurture it.

You have only one heart to take, mine.
Seize it.

We sat side by side in the morning light and looked out at the future together.

~ Brian Andres

WHERE HEARTS UNITE

When my eyes are too tired to stay open,
I close them, so I can imagine…

a family of turtles bathing in the sun in our yard,
the basket you attached to the bicycle, for our dog,
the orange juice you make right before breakfast,
a candle you light before we sit by the pond.

When my hands are too tired to stay clenched,
I open them, so I can feel…

a mug filled with coffee, sugar, and milk;
the softness of your feet on our bathroom floor;
the books that like snow cover your world
with white pages of wisdom, care, and faith.

When my mind is too tired to carry on,
I close the book, and I hear you…

locking all the doors and turning off all lights,
rearranging our bed—making it ready for sleep,
playing perfect music at the perfect volume,
so we can travel to a place where hearts unite.

Is it so small a thing
To have enjoy'd the sun,
To have lived light in the spring,
To have loved, to have thought,
to have done...

~ **Matthew Arnold**

I FEEL PEACEFUL

In the spring,
I feel peaceful when I look at a tree branch—
how new leaves open their arms to a life.

In the summer,
I feel peaceful when at the lake at dusk—
a mother loon announces our bedtime.

In the autumn,
I feel peaceful walking through the woods—
pushing rustling leaves with my feet.

In the winter,
I feel peaceful when, under melting snow,
a new life is reborn in our yard.

In my life,
I feel peaceful when, through all the seasons,
I have you to walk with me again and again.

CUANDO ESTOY CONTIGO*

Cuando estoy contigo
el tiempo no tiene relojes ni plazos.
Extiende cada momento por siempre.
La paz fluye por mis venas,
La inspiración sopla por mis pulmones,
Y el amor se queda en mi corazón.

Cuando estoy contigo
las estrellas descienden en la noche
y bailan a nuestro alrededor como ángeles de amor.
Los lamentos de aves adormecidas se mezclan
con el crujir de pinos ardientes
y nos rodean con tibieza en sus brazos
como una madre que abraza a sus hijos.

Cuando yo estoy contigo
Yo siento más,
Yo amo más,
Yo soy más.

* *(Spanish version)*

WHEN I AM WITH YOU

When I am with you
time has no clocks or deadlines.
It stretches each moment forever.
Peace flows through my veins.
Inspiration blows through my lungs.
And love settles in my heart.

When I am with you
stars lower themselves at night
and dance around us like angels of love.
The cries of sleepy loons mix
with the crackles of burning pines
and surround us with arms of warmth
like a mother embracing her children.

When I am with you
I feel more.
I love more.
I am more.

El amor es una elección que haces momento a momento.

~ Barbara De Angelis

*Love is a choice you make from
moment to moment.*

~ Barbara De Angelis

*It takes one person to forgive,
it takes two people to be reunited.*

~ Lewis B. Smedes

WE JUST COULD NOT END IT

It doesn't matter who called whom first,
or that your mom can't comprehend it.
Still, hours later, we kept on talking.
It seemed that we just could not end it.

You sounded apologetic at first.
But then your voice sounded strong.
Your "My" turned into "You"
and "sorry" to "You're wrong!"

You suggested couples therapy and books.
You said, "I know it all and understand it!"
I was so mad, but I couldn't hang up.
It seemed I just could not end it.

It was late at night when your voice broke
like a dropped glass on ceramic floor.
And in one heartbeat, one millisecond,
I was dressed and out the door.

Soon, I knocked on the window,
and you let me in—
back to your life and to our bed.
We let love win.

Goodness is the only investment that never fails.

~ **Henry David Thoreau**

PANCAKES MADE WITH YOUR SMILE

There you are,
smiling by the stove,
asking us what kind of pancakes we want.

We can have with chocolate chips or plain,
and as many of them as we can eat.

The youngest child cries for chocolaty, of course.
The oldest requests the plain ones.

When my turn comes to place an order,
I ask for those that have the flavor
of your lovingness,
friendliness,
peacefulness,
goodness,
devotion,
understanding,
patience,
wisdom,
and sensuality.

And only one type can be that versatile—
pancakes made with your smile.

*When you love someone,
all your saved-up wishes
start coming out.*

~ **Elizabeth Bowen**

WHAT I WOULDN'T GIVE

What I wouldn't give
to see you as a child playing on your mom's lap,
to see you in your high school classroom,
sitting in front of books, pencils, and friends,
sketching your hometown's sugar maples
that wave to you through a youthful window.

What I wouldn't give to be there with you,
to see you growing up, dreaming,
expecting life to be good.

What I wouldn't give to be there with you,
to protect you, laugh with you, dance with you,
to steal your first kiss.

What I wouldn't give to turn back time,
to stand on an American street at age sixteen,
hoping to be noticed by a girl like you.
What I wouldn't give.

*We have more possibilities available
in each moment than we realize.*

~ Thich Nhat Hanh

YOU CAN

You manage to find the only straight thread
in a fabric of entangled tasks,
and to hear a quiet word
in loud sentences of pointless arguments.

You are able to find a colorful photo
in the black and white pages of life,
and to point to a shining star
in a never-ending darkness of memories.

You are skilled in throwing a chance
across the field of opportunity,
and hiding your newly healed pain
when an unwanted phone call arrives.

You can turn dreams to reality,
a touch of knees to kneeling,
a smile to laughter, and a fear of living
to living happily ever after.

Aquél que ama, cree lo imposible.

~ Elizabeth Barrett Browning

Whoso loves, believes the impossible.

~ **Elizabeth Barrett Browning**

*I dropped a tear in the ocean.
The day you find it is the day
I will stop missing you.*

~ Author Unknown

WHEN I MISS YOU

Food turns tasteless,
water dries my mouth,
mind replays what ears hear, but ignore.

Neighbors seem distant,
your parents speak louder,
dog sleeps lighter and gazes at the door.

The clock ticks slower,
plants bloom rarer,
the mailman arrives on every other day.

Days seem longer,
nights are endless,
"I wish you were here," I pray, I pray.

*There is only one happiness in life,
to love and be loved.*

~ George Sand

DISCOVERING YOU

Like a magic eye, I hope to perceive you
hidden in a picture made of my life's illusions
where colors of love, trust, and happiness
compose your three-dimensional image.

With an attentive ear, I hope to hear your heart beat,
a heart petrified from giving "No!" for an answer,
longing for unconditional love,
divided into pieces like Jesus' bread,
misread as insufficient but able to feed all.

With perceptive eyes I hope to discover
a new smile on your lips,
a new movement of your hands,
a new wrinkle on your face,
an uninvited gray hair on your head.

I hope to discover something new in you, forever.

And when I'm old,
with trembling hands
but cloudless consciousness,
I hope to complete my search and say,
"I found you."

My heart to you is given:
Oh, do give yours to me;
We'll lock them up together,
And throw away the key.

~ Frederick Saunders

WILL YOU BE MY AIR?

There is no gentler sound to sleepy trees
than to hear the wind's easy breeze.
There is no better hope to a love-starved soul
than to find someone precious, to feel whole.

There is no better road, no better endeavor
than the one for better, for worse, forever.
Dear beloved*, you're my soul, my prayer.
For as long as I breathe, you will be my air.

* or insert name

*If I had to choose between
loving you and breathing.
I would use my last breath to say
I love you.*

~ **Author unknown**

I WILL BE YOUR AIR

There is no better gift to meadows and flowers
than the soft clean flow of early spring showers.
There is no better feeling to a drop of rain
than to hear the other drops' splashing refrain.

There is no better road, no better endeavor
than the one for better, for worse, forever.
Dear beloved*, you're my soul, my prayer.
For as long as you breathe, I will be your air.

* or insert name

FINAL NOTE

My wish is that you find hope in *In Love*—the kind of hope that gives us strength when we need it in times of loneliness or sadness, in times of worry and doubt, in times of the tests with which life seems to frequently surprise us.

In Love was written with great contentment and satisfaction. After all, it was written...in love.

Please share your comments and love stories. Visit my website for other books, articles, and presentations at:

www.1moment.us

Chez